D0514324

THE GOSPEL OF MARK

CHRISTIANITY|**EXPLORED**

NIV

This edition of the NIV Gospel of Mark is
published by The Good Book Company, 2016.

The Good Book Company Ltd.
Blenheim House, 1 Blenheim Road
Epsom, Surrey KT19 9AP, UK
Tel: 0333 123 0880
International: +44 (0) 208 942 0880
Email: info@thegoodbook.co.uk

Websites:
UK: www.thegoodbook.co.uk
North America: www.thegoodbook.com
Australia: www.thegoodbook.com.au
New Zealand: www.thegoodbook.co.nz

CHRISTIANITY
EXPLORED
M I N I S T R I E S

ISBN (single): 9781784981440
ISBN (pack of 20): 9781784981457

Scripture taken from the Holy Bible, New International Version.
Copyright © 1973, 1978, 1984, 2011 by Biblica. Used by permission of
Zondervan. All rights reserved.

Used by permission of Hodder & Stoughton Publishers, a division of
Hachette UK
All rights reserved.

"NIV" is a registered trade mark of International Bible Society.
UK trade mark number 1448790.

First published in the UK by Hodder & Stoughton Publishers.

All additional material © Christianity Explored Ministries 2011

www.christianityexplored.org

Printed in India

READ THIS FIRST

You have just opened a truly remarkable book.

It tells the extraordinary story of the most influential man who ever lived – Jesus Christ. It's a story that is both heart-warming and shocking. It's a story that people died to write down and preserve so that you can hold it in your hands today and read it. It's a story that has changed the lives of countless people around the world and throughout history.

Most of us will have heard something about Jesus, and know some of the details of his life and teaching. Perhaps you listened to some stories about Jesus when you were a child. Or maybe you learned something about him at school. But many people have never taken time as an adult to examine Jesus—to consider the meaning of the man from Galilee from a mature viewpoint.

The book you are holding is a great place to start. It was written by a man called Mark, who researched his information from people who were eyewitnesses of the life and death of Jesus. These same eyewitnesses were also there when the astonishing events of the first Easter unfolded. Mark writes his book knowing it to be the truth – not made-up stories, but history.

Mark's Gospel is the shortest of four accounts of the life of Jesus in the Bible. The word "Gospel" means "good news". These people that wrote the Gospels were convinced that Jesus was good news for the whole world.

In his opening words, Mark tells us what this good news is that he wants to share with us: it is about Jesus the Messiah, the Son of God. It is about the identity of Jesus.

So can we encourage you to read this book with an open mind, and an open heart? As you read it, ask the question that Mark asks: Who is Jesus? You may be surprised by what you discover…

SOME PRACTICAL SUGGESTIONS

Read it slowly...

You can read through Mark's Gospel in less than two hours. But to really think about what Mark is saying about Jesus, it is better to take it slowly. Use the reading plan on page 6 to work your way through a bit at a time.

Read it thoughtfully...

Many of the stories Jesus told were a bit like puzzles. The people at the time didn't "get them" immediately. So rather than speeding through to get to the end, take time to pause and think about the meaning of the stories and incidents. Because Mark's Gospel is so old, there are details that may be unfamiliar to you. There is a map on page 63 to show you where the events described in Mark happened.

Read it responsively...

There's a short section in the middle to help you think about some of the things raised in the first half. And after you have finished Mark there is a section at the back – on page 55 – that explains how you might respond to what you have read. And finally...

Read it prayerfully...

Mark wrote his Gospel because he had found forgiveness and new meaning in life through Jesus. Wherever you are on your spiritual journey, God wants to help you understand what you are reading. He is willing to answer even the most faltering prayer. The words below may help you.

A PRAYER TO USE BEFORE READING MARK

Lord God, please help me as I read Mark's Gospel.
Help me to understand why what he has written is good news.
Help me to understand who Jesus is and what he achieved.
Help me to understand the parts that I find difficult,
and above all help me to respond to Jesus in the right way.

Amen.

THE GOSPEL OF MARK

A READING PLAN: MARK IN THREE WEEKS

You can read through Mark's Gospel in less than two hours. But to really think about what he is telling us about Jesus, it is better to take it slowly. Use the reading plan below to work your way through Mark, taking time to think about what you read.

☐ Day 1. Mark 1:1-28

☐ Day 2. Mark 1:29 – 2:12

☐ Day 3. Mark 2:13 – 3:6

☐ Day 4. Mark 3:7-34

☐ Day 5. Mark 4:1-41

☐ Day 6. Mark 5:1-20

☐ Day 7. Mark 5:21-43

☐ Day 8. Mark 6:1-29

☐ Day 9. Mark 6:30-56

☐ Day 10. Mark 7:1-37

☐ Day 11. Mark 8:1-38

☐ Day 12. Mark 9:1-32

☐ Day 13. Mark 9:33 – 10:16

☐ Day 14. Mark 10:17-52

☐ Day 15. Mark 11:1-33

☐ Day 16. Mark 12:1-44

☐ Day 17. Mark 13:1-37

☐ Day 18. Mark 14:1-52

☐ Day 19. Mark 14:53 – 15:15

☐ Day 20. Mark 15:16-47

☐ Day 21. Mark 16

A note about chapters and verses

Throughout this book you will see some large numbers and some smaller numbers. The larger numbers are chapters that Mark has been split into. The smaller numbers are the verses that make up each chapter. The chapters and verses weren't in the original but have been added later to help us find our way around. We often use a kind of shorthand so that Mark chapter 1 and verse 1 will be written as "Mark 1:1" or sometimes as "Mark 1 v 1".

John the Baptist prepares the way

1 The beginning of the good news about Jesus the Messiah,[a] the Son of God,[b] [2] as it is written in Isaiah the prophet:

> *'I will send my messenger ahead of you,*
> *who will prepare your way'*[c] –
> [3] *'a voice of one calling in the wilderness,*
> *"Prepare the way for the Lord,*
> *make straight paths for him."'*[d]

[4] And so John the Baptist appeared in the wilderness, preaching a baptism of repentance for the forgiveness of sins. [5] The whole Judean countryside and all the people of Jerusalem went out to him. Confessing their sins, they were baptised by him in the River Jordan. [6] John wore clothing made of camel's hair, with a leather belt round his waist, and he ate locusts and wild honey. [7] And this was his message: 'After me comes the one more powerful than I, the straps of whose sandals I am not worthy to stoop down and untie. [8] I baptise you with[e] water, but he will baptise you with[e] the Holy Spirit.'

The baptism and testing of Jesus

[9] At that time Jesus came from Nazareth in Galilee and was baptised by John in the Jordan. [10] Just as Jesus was coming up out of the water, he saw heaven being torn open and the Spirit descending on him like a dove. [11] And a voice came from heaven: 'You are my Son, whom I love; with you I am well pleased.'

[12] At once the Spirit sent him out into the wilderness, [13] and

a 1 Or *Jesus Christ. Messiah* (Hebrew) and *Christ* (Greek) both mean *Anointed One.*
b 1 Some manuscripts do not have *the Son of God.*
c 2 Mal. 3:1
d 3 Isaiah 40:3
e 8 Or *in*

he was in the wilderness for forty days, being tempted[f] by Satan. He was with the wild animals, and angels attended him.

Jesus announces the good news

14 After John was put in prison, Jesus went into Galilee, proclaiming the good news of God. 15 'The time has come,' he said. 'The kingdom of God has come near. Repent and believe the good news!'

Jesus calls his first disciples

16 As Jesus walked beside the Sea of Galilee, he saw Simon and his brother Andrew casting a net into the lake, for they were fishermen. 17 'Come, follow me,' Jesus said, 'and I will send you out to fish for people.' 18 At once they left their nets and followed him.

19 When he had gone a little farther, he saw James son of Zebedee and his brother John in a boat, preparing their nets. 20 Without delay he called them, and they left their father Zebedee in the boat with the hired men and followed him.

Jesus drives out an impure spirit

21 They went to Capernaum, and when the Sabbath came, Jesus went into the synagogue and began to teach. 22 The people were amazed at his teaching, because he taught them as one who had authority, not as the teachers of the law. 23 Just then a man in their synagogue who was possessed by an impure spirit cried out, 24 'What do you want with us, Jesus of Nazareth? Have you come to destroy us? I know who you are – the Holy One of God!'

25 'Be quiet!' said Jesus sternly. 'Come out of him!' 26 The impure spirit shook the man violently and came out of him with a shriek.

27 The people were all so amazed that they asked each other, 'What is this? A new teaching – and with authority! He even gives orders to impure spirits and they obey him.' 28 News about him spread quickly over the whole region of Galilee.

f 13 The Greek for *tempted* can also mean *tested*.

Jesus heals many

²⁹ As soon as they left the synagogue, they went with James and John to the home of Simon and Andrew. ³⁰ Simon's mother-in-law was in bed with a fever, and they immediately told Jesus about her. ³¹ So he went to her, took her hand and helped her up. The fever left her and she began to wait on them.

³² That evening after sunset the people brought to Jesus all who were ill and demon-possessed. ³³ The whole town gathered at the door, ³⁴ and Jesus healed many who had various diseases. He also drove out many demons, but he would not let the demons speak because they knew who he was.

Jesus prays in a solitary place

³⁵ Very early in the morning, while it was still dark, Jesus got up, left the house and went off to a solitary place, where he prayed. ³⁶ Simon and his companions went to look for him, ³⁷ and when they found him, they exclaimed: 'Everyone is looking for you!'

³⁸ Jesus replied, 'Let us go somewhere else – to the nearby villages – so that I can preach there also. That is why I have come.' ³⁹ So he travelled throughout Galilee, preaching in their synagogues and driving out demons.

Jesus heals a man with leprosy

⁴⁰ A man with leprosyᵍ came to him and begged him on his knees, 'If you are willing, you can make me clean.'

⁴¹ Jesus was indignant.ʰ He reached out his hand and touched the man. 'I am willing,' he said. 'Be clean!' ⁴² Immediately the leprosy left him and he was cleansed.

⁴³ Jesus sent him away at once with a strong warning: ⁴⁴ 'See that you don't tell this to anyone. But go, show yourself to the priest and offer the sacrifices that Moses commanded for your cleansing, as a testimony to them.' ⁴⁵ Instead he went out and began to talk freely, spreading the news. As a result, Jesus could no longer enter a town openly but stayed outside

g 40 The Greek word traditionally translated *leprosy* was used for various diseases affecting the skin.
h 41 Many manuscripts *Jesus was filled with compassion*

in lonely places. Yet the people still came to him from everywhere.

Jesus forgives and heals a paralysed man

2 A few days later, when Jesus again entered Capernaum, the people heard that he had come home. ²They gathered in such large numbers that there was no room left, not even outside the door, and he preached the word to them. ³Some men came, bringing to him a paralysed man, carried by four of them. ⁴Since they could not get him to Jesus because of the crowd, they made an opening in the roof above Jesus by digging through it and then lowered the mat the man was lying on. ⁵When Jesus saw their faith, he said to the paralysed man, 'Son, your sins are forgiven.'

⁶Now some teachers of the law were sitting there, thinking to themselves, ⁷'Why does this fellow talk like that? He's blaspheming! Who can forgive sins but God alone?'

⁸Immediately Jesus knew in his spirit that this was what they were thinking in their hearts, and he said to them, 'Why are you thinking these things? ⁹Which is easier: to say to this paralysed man, "Your sins are forgiven," or to say, "Get up, take your mat and walk"? ¹⁰But I want you to know that the Son of Man has authority on earth to forgive sins.' So he said to the man, ¹¹'I tell you, get up, take your mat and go home.' ¹²He got up, took his mat and walked out in full view of them all. This amazed everyone and they praised God, saying, 'We have never seen anything like this!'

Jesus calls Levi and eats with sinners

¹³Once again Jesus went out beside the lake. A large crowd came to him, and he began to teach them. ¹⁴As he walked along, he saw Levi son of Alphaeus sitting at the tax collector's booth. 'Follow me,' Jesus told him, and Levi got up and followed him.

¹⁵While Jesus was having dinner at Levi's house, many tax collectors and sinners were eating with him and his disciples,

for there were many who followed him. ¹⁶When the teachers of the law who were Pharisees saw him eating with the sinners and tax collectors, they asked his disciples: 'Why does he eat with tax collectors and sinners?'

¹⁷On hearing this, Jesus said to them, 'It is not the healthy who need a doctor, but those who are ill. I have not come to call the righteous, but sinners.'

Jesus questioned about fasting

¹⁸Now John's disciples and the Pharisees were fasting. Some people came and asked Jesus, 'How is it that John's disciples and the disciples of the Pharisees are fasting, but yours are not?'

¹⁹Jesus answered, 'How can the guests of the bridegroom fast while he is with them? They cannot, so long as they have him with them. ²⁰But the time will come when the bridegroom will be taken from them, and on that day they will fast.

²¹'No one sews a patch of unshrunk cloth on an old garment. Otherwise, the new piece will pull away from the old, making the tear worse. ²²And no one pours new wine into old wineskins. Otherwise, the wine will burst the skins, and both the wine and the wineskins will be ruined. No, they pour new wine into new wineskins.'

Jesus is Lord of the Sabbath

²³One Sabbath Jesus was going through the cornfields, and as his disciples walked along, they began to pick some ears of corn. ²⁴The Pharisees said to him, 'Look, why are they doing what is unlawful on the Sabbath?'

²⁵He answered, 'Have you never read what David did when he and his companions were hungry and in need? ²⁶In the days of Abiathar the high priest, he entered the house of God and ate the consecrated bread, which is lawful only for priests to eat. And he also gave some to his companions.'

²⁷Then he said to them, 'The Sabbath was made for man,

not man for the Sabbath. ²⁸So the Son of Man is Lord even of the Sabbath.'

Jesus heals on the Sabbath

3 Another time Jesus went into the synagogue, and a man with a shrivelled hand was there. ²Some of them were looking for a reason to accuse Jesus, so they watched him closely to see if he would heal him on the Sabbath. ³Jesus said to the man with the shrivelled hand, 'Stand up in front of everyone.'

⁴Then Jesus asked them, 'Which is lawful on the Sabbath: to do good or to do evil, to save life or to kill?' But they remained silent.

⁵He looked around at them in anger and, deeply distressed at their stubborn hearts, said to the man, 'Stretch out your hand.' He stretched it out, and his hand was completely restored. ⁶Then the Pharisees went out and began to plot with the Herodians how they might kill Jesus.

Crowds follow Jesus

⁷Jesus withdrew with his disciples to the lake, and a large crowd from Galilee followed. ⁸When they heard all he was doing, many people came to him from Judea, Jerusalem, Idumea, and the regions across the Jordan and around Tyre and Sidon. ⁹Because of the crowd he told his disciples to have a small boat ready for him, to keep the people from crowding him. ¹⁰For he had healed many, so that those with diseases were pushing forward to touch him. ¹¹Whenever the impure spirits saw him, they fell down before him and cried out, 'You are the Son of God.' ¹²But he gave them strict orders not to tell others about him.

Jesus appoints the Twelve

¹³Jesus went up on a mountainside and called to him those he wanted, and they came to him. ¹⁴He appointed twelve^a that they might be with him and that he might send them out to

---

a 14 Some manuscripts *twelve – designating them apostles –*

preach ¹⁵ and to have authority to drive out demons. ¹⁶These are the twelve he appointed: Simon (to whom he gave the name Peter); ¹⁷James son of Zebedee and his brother John (to them he gave the name Boanerges, which means 'sons of thunder'), ¹⁸Andrew, Philip, Bartholomew, Matthew, Thomas, James son of Alphaeus, Thaddaeus, Simon the Zealot ¹⁹and Judas Iscariot, who betrayed him.

Jesus accused by his family and by teachers of the law

²⁰Then Jesus entered a house, and again a crowd gathered, so that he and his disciples were not even able to eat. ²¹When his family^b heard about this, they went to take charge of him, for they said, 'He is out of his mind.'

²²And the teachers of the law who came down from Jerusalem said, 'He is possessed by Beelzebul! By the prince of demons he is driving out demons.'

²³So Jesus called them over to him and began to speak to them in parables: 'How can Satan drive out Satan? ²⁴If a kingdom is divided against itself, that kingdom cannot stand. ²⁵If a house is divided against itself, that house cannot stand. ²⁶And if Satan opposes himself and is divided, he cannot stand; his end has come. ²⁷In fact, no one can enter a strong man's house without first tying him up. Then he can plunder the strong man's house. ²⁸Truly I tell you, people can be forgiven all their sins and every slander they utter, ²⁹but whoever blasphemes against the Holy Spirit will never be forgiven; they are guilty of an eternal sin.'

³⁰He said this because they were saying, 'He has an impure spirit.'

³¹Then Jesus' mother and brothers arrived. Standing outside, they sent someone in to call him. ³²A crowd was sitting round him, and they told him, 'Your mother and brothers are outside looking for you.'

³³'Who are my mother and my brothers?' he asked.

³⁴Then he looked at those seated in a circle round him and

said, 'Here are my mother and my brothers! ³⁵Whoever does God's will is my brother and sister and mother.'

The parable of the sower

4 Again Jesus began to teach by the lake. The crowd that gathered round him was so large that he got into a boat and sat in it out on the lake, while all the people were along the shore at the water's edge. ²He taught them many things by parables, and in his teaching said: ³'Listen! A farmer went out to sow his seed. ⁴As he was scattering the seed, some fell along the path, and the birds came and ate it up. ⁵Some fell on rocky places, where it did not have much soil. It sprang up quickly, because the soil was shallow. ⁶But when the sun came up, the plants were scorched, and they withered because they had no root. ⁷Other seed fell among thorns, which grew up and choked the plants, so that they did not bear grain. ⁸Still other seed fell on good soil. It came up, grew and produced a crop, some multiplying thirty, some sixty, some a hundred times.'

⁹Then Jesus said, 'Whoever has ears to hear, let them hear.'

¹⁰When he was alone, the Twelve and the others around him asked him about the parables. ¹¹He told them, 'The secret of the kingdom of God has been given to you. But to those on the outside everything is said in parables ¹²so that,

> '"they may be ever seeing but never perceiving,
>   and ever hearing but never understanding;
>   otherwise they might turn and be forgiven!"ᵃ'

¹³Then Jesus said to them, 'Don't you understand this parable? How then will you understand any parable? ¹⁴The farmer sows the word. ¹⁵Some people are like seed along the path, where the word is sown. As soon as they hear it, Satan comes and takes away the word that was sown in them. ¹⁶Others, like seed sown on rocky places, hear the word and at once receive it with joy. ¹⁷But since they have no root, they last only

a 12 Isaiah 6:9,10

a short time. When trouble or persecution comes because of the word, they quickly fall away. [18]Still others, like seed sown among thorns, hear the word; [19]but the worries of this life, the deceitfulness of wealth and the desires for other things come in and choke the word, making it unfruitful. [20]Others, like seed sown on good soil, hear the word, accept it, and produce a crop – some thirty, some sixty, some a hundred times what was sown.'

A lamp on a stand

[21]He said to them, 'Do you bring in a lamp to put it under a bowl or a bed? Instead, don't you put it on its stand? [22]For whatever is hidden is meant to be disclosed, and whatever is concealed is meant to be brought out into the open. [23]If anyone has ears to hear, let them hear.'

[24]'Consider carefully what you hear,' he continued. 'With the measure you use, it will be measured to you – and even more. [25]Whoever has will be given more; whoever does not have, even what they have will be taken from them.'

The parable of the growing seed

[26]He also said, 'This is what the kingdom of God is like. A man scatters seed on the ground. [27]Night and day, whether he sleeps or gets up, the seed sprouts and grows, though he does not know how. [28]All by itself the soil produces corn – first the stalk, then the ear, then the full grain in the ear. [29]As soon as the corn is ripe, he puts the sickle to it, because the harvest has come.'

The parable of the mustard seed

[30]Again he said, 'What shall we say the kingdom of God is like, or what parable shall we use to describe it? [31]It is like a mustard seed, which is the smallest of all seeds on earth. [32]Yet when planted, it grows and becomes the largest of all garden plants, with such big branches that the birds can perch in its shade.'

³³With many similar parables Jesus spoke the word to them, as much as they could understand. ³⁴He did not say anything to them without using a parable. But when he was alone with his own disciples, he explained everything.

Jesus calms the storm

³⁵That day when evening came, he said to his disciples, 'Let us go over to the other side.' ³⁶Leaving the crowd behind, they took him along, just as he was, in the boat. There were also other boats with him. ³⁷A furious squall came up, and the waves broke over the boat, so that it was nearly swamped. ³⁸Jesus was in the stern, sleeping on a cushion. The disciples woke him and said to him, 'Teacher, don't you care if we drown?'

³⁹He got up, rebuked the wind and said to the waves, 'Quiet! Be still!' Then the wind died down and it was completely calm.

⁴⁰He said to his disciples, 'Why are you so afraid? Do you still have no faith?'

⁴¹They were terrified and asked each other, 'Who is this? Even the wind and the waves obey him!'

Jesus restores a demon-possessed man

5 They went across the lake to the region of the Gerasenes.ᵃ ²When Jesus got out of the boat, a man with an impure spirit came from the tombs to meet him. ³This man lived in the tombs, and no one could bind him anymore, not even with a chain. ⁴For he had often been chained hand and foot, but he tore the chains apart and broke the irons on his feet. No one was strong enough to subdue him. ⁵Night and day among the tombs and in the hills he would cry out and cut himself with stones.

⁶When he saw Jesus from a distance, he ran and fell on his knees in front of him. ⁷He shouted at the top of his voice, 'What do you want with me, Jesus, Son of the Most High God? In God's name don't torture me!' ⁸For Jesus had said to him, 'Come out of this man, you impure spirit!'

a 1 Some manuscripts *Gadarenes*; other manuscripts *Gergesenes*

⁹Then Jesus asked him, 'What is your name?'

'My name is Legion,' he replied, 'for we are many.' ¹⁰And he begged Jesus again and again not to send them out of the area.

¹¹A large herd of pigs was feeding on the nearby hillside. ¹²The demons begged Jesus, 'Send us among the pigs; allow us to go into them.' ¹³He gave them permission, and the impure spirits came out and went into the pigs. The herd, about two thousand in number, rushed down the steep bank into the lake and were drowned.

¹⁴Those tending the pigs ran off and reported this in the town and countryside, and the people went out to see what had happened. ¹⁵When they came to Jesus, they saw the man who had been possessed by the legion of demons, sitting there, dressed and in his right mind; and they were afraid. ¹⁶Those who had seen it told the people what had happened to the demon-possessed man – and told about the pigs as well. ¹⁷Then the people began to plead with Jesus to leave their region.

¹⁸As Jesus was getting into the boat, the man who had been demon-possessed begged to go with him. ¹⁹Jesus did not let him, but said, 'Go home to your own people and tell them how much the Lord has done for you, and how he has had mercy on you.' ²⁰So the man went away and began to tell in the Decapolisᵇ how much Jesus had done for him. And all the people were amazed.

Jesus raises a dead girl and heals a sick woman

²¹When Jesus had again crossed over by boat to the other side of the lake, a large crowd gathered round him while he was by the lake. ²²Then one of the synagogue leaders, named Jairus, came, and when he saw Jesus, he fell at his feet. ²³He pleaded earnestly with him, 'My little daughter is dying. Please come and put your hands on her so that she will be healed and live.' ²⁴So Jesus went with him.

A large crowd followed and pressed round him. ²⁵And a woman was there who had been subject to bleeding for twelve

b 20 That is, the Ten Cities

years. 26 She had suffered a great deal under the care of many doctors and had spent all she had, yet instead of getting better she grew worse. 27 When she heard about Jesus, she came up behind him in the crowd and touched his cloak, 28 because she thought, 'If I just touch his clothes, I will be healed.' 29 Immediately her bleeding stopped and she felt in her body that she was freed from her suffering.

30 At once Jesus realised that power had gone out from him. He turned round in the crowd and asked, 'Who touched my clothes?'

31 'You see the people crowding against you,' his disciples answered, 'and yet you can ask, "Who touched me?" '

32 But Jesus kept looking around to see who had done it. 33 Then the woman, knowing what had happened to her, came and fell at his feet and, trembling with fear, told him the whole truth. 34 He said to her, 'Daughter, your faith has healed you. Go in peace and be freed from your suffering.'

35 While Jesus was still speaking, some people came from the house of Jairus, the synagogue leader. 'Your daughter is dead,' they said. 'Why bother the teacher anymore?'

36 Overhearing c what they said, Jesus told him, 'Don't be afraid; just believe.'

37 He did not let anyone follow him except Peter, James and John the brother of James. 38 When they came to the home of the synagogue leader, Jesus saw a commotion, with people crying and wailing loudly. 39 He went in and said to them, 'Why all this commotion and wailing? The child is not dead but asleep.' 40 But they laughed at him.

After he put them all out, he took the child's father and mother and the disciples who were with him, and went in where the child was. 41 He took her by the hand and said to her, 'Talitha koum!' (which means 'Little girl, I say to you, get up!'). 42 Immediately the girl stood up and began to walk around (she was twelve years old). At this they were completely astonished. 43 He gave strict orders not to let anyone know about this, and told them to give her something to eat.

c 36 Or *Ignoring*

A prophet without honour

6 Jesus left there and went to his home town, accompanied by his disciples. ²When the Sabbath came, he began to teach in the synagogue, and many who heard him were amazed.

'Where did this man get these things?' they asked. 'What's this wisdom that has been given him? What are these remarkable miracles he is performing? ³Isn't this the carpenter? Isn't this Mary's son and the brother of James, Joseph,ª Judas and Simon? Aren't his sisters here with us?' And they took offence at him.

⁴Jesus said to them, 'A prophet is not without honour except in his own town, among his relatives and in his own home.' ⁵He could not do any miracles there, except lay his hands on a few people who were ill and heal them. ⁶He was amazed at their lack of faith.

Jesus sends out the Twelve

Then Jesus went around teaching from village to village. ⁷Calling the Twelve to him, he began to send them out two by two and gave them authority over impure spirits.

⁸These were his instructions: 'Take nothing for the journey except a staff – no bread, no bag, no money in your belts. ⁹Wear sandals but not an extra shirt. ¹⁰Whenever you enter a house, stay there until you leave that town. ¹¹And if any place will not welcome you or listen to you, leave that place and shake the dust off your feet as a testimony against them.'

¹²They went out and preached that people should repent. ¹³They drove out many demons and anointed with oil many people who were ill and healed them.

John the Baptist beheaded

¹⁴King Herod heard about this, for Jesus' name had become well known. Some were saying,ᵇ 'John the Baptist has been raised from the dead, and that is why miraculous powers are at work in him.'

¹⁵Others said, 'He is Elijah.'

a 3 Greek *Joses*, a variant of *Joseph*
b 14 Some early manuscripts *He was saying*

And still others claimed, 'He is a prophet, like one of the prophets of long ago.'

¹⁶But when Herod heard this, he said, 'John, whom I beheaded, has been raised from the dead!'

¹⁷For Herod himself had given orders to have John arrested, and he had him bound and put in prison. He did this because of Herodias, his brother Philip's wife, whom he had married. ¹⁸For John had been saying to Herod, 'It is not lawful for you to have your brother's wife.' ¹⁹So Herodias nursed a grudge against John and wanted to kill him. But she was not able to, ²⁰because Herod feared John and protected him, knowing him to be a righteous and holy man. When Herod heard John, he was greatly puzzled^c; yet he liked to listen to him.

²¹Finally the opportune time came. On his birthday Herod gave a banquet for his high officials and military commanders and the leading men of Galilee. ²²When the daughter of^d Herodias came in and danced, she pleased Herod and his dinner guests.

The king said to the girl, 'Ask me for anything you want, and I'll give it to you.' ²³And he promised her with an oath, 'Whatever you ask I will give you, up to half my kingdom.'

²⁴She went out and said to her mother, 'What shall I ask for?'

'The head of John the Baptist,' she answered.

²⁵At once the girl hurried in to the king with the request: 'I want you to give me right now the head of John the Baptist on a dish.'

²⁶The king was greatly distressed, but because of his oaths and his dinner guests, he did not want to refuse her. ²⁷So he immediately sent an executioner with orders to bring John's head. The man went, beheaded John in the prison, ²⁸and brought back his head on a dish. He presented it to the girl, and she gave it to her mother. ²⁹On hearing of this, John's disciples came and took his body and laid it in a tomb.

---

c 20 Some early manuscripts *he did many things*
d 22 Some early manuscripts *When his daughter*

Jesus feeds the five thousand

³⁰The apostles gathered round Jesus and reported to him all they had done and taught. ³¹Then, because so many people were coming and going that they did not even have a chance to eat, he said to them, 'Come with me by yourselves to a quiet place and get some rest.'

³²So they went away by themselves in a boat to a solitary place. ³³But many who saw them leaving recognised them and ran on foot from all the towns and got there ahead of them. ³⁴When Jesus landed and saw a large crowd, he had compassion on them, because they were like sheep without a shepherd. So he began teaching them many things.

³⁵By this time it was late in the day, so his disciples came to him. 'This is a remote place,' they said, 'and it's already very late. ³⁶Send the people away so that they can go to the surrounding countryside and villages and buy themselves something to eat.'

³⁷But he answered, 'You give them something to eat.'

They said to him, 'That would take more than half a year's wagesᵉ! Are we to go and spend that much on bread and give it to them to eat?'

³⁸'How many loaves do you have?' he asked. 'Go and see.'

When they found out, they said, 'Five – and two fish.'

³⁹Then Jesus told them to make all the people sit down in groups on the green grass. ⁴⁰So they sat down in groups of hundreds and fifties. ⁴¹Taking the five loaves and the two fish and looking up to heaven, he gave thanks and broke the loaves. Then he gave them to his disciples to distribute to the people. He also divided the two fish among them all. ⁴²They all ate and were satisfied, ⁴³and the disciples picked up twelve basketfuls of broken pieces of bread and fish. ⁴⁴The number of the men who had eaten was five thousand.

Jesus walks on the water

⁴⁵Immediately Jesus made his disciples get into the boat and

go on ahead of him to Bethsaida, while he dismissed the crowd. ⁴⁶After leaving them, he went up on a mountainside to pray.

⁴⁷Later that night, the boat was in the middle of the lake, and he was alone on land. ⁴⁸He saw the disciples straining at the oars, because the wind was against them. Shortly before dawn he went out to them, walking on the lake. He was about to pass by them, ⁴⁹but when they saw him walking on the lake, they thought he was a ghost. They cried out, ⁵⁰because they all saw him and were terrified.

Immediately he spoke to them and said, 'Take courage! It is I. Don't be afraid.' ⁵¹Then he climbed into the boat with them, and the wind died down. They were completely amazed, ⁵²for they had not understood about the loaves; their hearts were hardened.

⁵³When they had crossed over, they landed at Gennesaret and anchored there. ⁵⁴As soon as they got out of the boat, people recognised Jesus. ⁵⁵They ran throughout that whole region and carried those who were ill on mats to wherever they heard he was. ⁵⁶And wherever he went – into villages, towns or countryside – they placed those who were ill in the market-places. They begged him to let them touch even the edge of his cloak, and all who touched it were healed.

That which defiles

7 The Pharisees and some of the teachers of the law who had come from Jerusalem gathered round Jesus ²and saw some of his disciples eating food with hands that were defiled, that is, unwashed. ³(The Pharisees and all the Jews do not eat unless they give their hands a ceremonial washing, holding to the tradition of the elders. ⁴When they come from the market-place they do not eat unless they wash. And they observe many other traditions, such as the washing of cups, pitchers and kettles.ᵃ)

⁵So the Pharisees and teachers of the law asked Jesus, 'Why don't your disciples live according to the tradition of the elders instead of eating their food with defiled hands?'

a 4 Some early manuscripts *pitchers, kettles and dining couches*

⁶He replied, 'Isaiah was right when he prophesied about you hypocrites; as it is written:

' *"These people honour me with their lips,*
  but their hearts are far from me.
⁷ *They worship me in vain;*
  their teachings are merely human rules." b

⁸You have let go of the commands of God and are holding on to human traditions.'

⁹And he continued, 'You have a fine way of setting aside the commands of God in order to observe c your own traditions! ¹⁰For Moses said, "Honour your father and mother," d and, "Anyone who curses their father or mother is to be put to death." e ¹¹But you say that if anyone declares that what might have been used to help their father or mother is Corban (that is, devoted to God) – ¹²then you no longer let them do anything for their father or mother. ¹³Thus you nullify the word of God by your tradition that you have handed down. And you do many things like that.'

¹⁴Again Jesus called the crowd to him and said, 'Listen to me, everyone, and understand this. ¹⁵Nothing outside a person can defile them by going into them. Rather, it is what comes out of a person that defiles them.' [16] f

¹⁷After he had left the crowd and entered the house, his disciples asked him about this parable. ¹⁸'Are you so dull?' he asked. 'Don't you see that nothing that enters a person from the outside can defile them? ¹⁹For it doesn't go into their heart but into their stomach, and then out of the body.' (In saying this, Jesus declared all foods clean.)

²⁰He went on: 'What comes out of a person is what defiles them. ²¹For it is from within, out of a person's heart, that evil thoughts come – sexual immorality, theft, murder, ²²adultery,

b 6,7 Isaiah 29:13
c 9 Some manuscripts set up
d 10 Exodus 20:12; Deut. 5:16
e 10 Exodus 21:17; Lev. 20:9
f 16 Some manuscripts include here the words of 4:23.

greed, malice, deceit, lewdness, envy, slander, arrogance and folly. 23All these evils come from inside and defile a person.'

Jesus honours a Syro-Phoenician woman's faith

24Jesus left that place and went to the vicinity of Tyre.g He entered a house and did not want anyone to know it; yet he could not keep his presence secret. 25In fact, as soon as she heard about him, a woman whose little daughter was possessed by an impure spirit came and fell at his feet. 26The woman was a Greek, born in Syrian Phoenicia. She begged Jesus to drive the demon out of her daughter.

27'First let the children eat all they want,' he told her, 'for it is not right to take the children's bread and toss it to the dogs.'

28'Lord,' she replied, 'even the dogs under the table eat the children's crumbs.'

29Then he told her, 'For such a reply, you may go; the demon has left your daughter.'

30She went home and found her child lying on the bed, and the demon gone.

Jesus heals a deaf and mute man

31Then Jesus left the vicinity of Tyre and went through Sidon, down to the Sea of Galilee and into the region of the Decapolis.h 32There some people brought to him a man who was deaf and could hardly talk, and they begged Jesus to place his hand on him.

33After he took him aside, away from the crowd, Jesus put his fingers into the man's ears. Then he spat and touched the man's tongue. 34He looked up to heaven and with a deep sigh said to him, *'Ephphatha!'* (which means 'Be opened!'). 35At this, the man's ears were opened, his tongue was loosed and he began to speak plainly.

36Jesus commanded them not to tell anyone. But the more he did so, the more they kept talking about it. 37People were overwhelmed with amazement. 'He has done everything well,' they said. 'He even makes the deaf hear and the mute speak.'

g 24 Many early manuscripts *Tyre and Sidon*
h 31 That is, the Ten Cities

Jesus feeds the four thousand

8 During those days another large crowd gathered. Since they had nothing to eat, Jesus called his disciples to him and said, 2'I have compassion for these people; they have already been with me three days and have nothing to eat. 3If I send them home hungry, they will collapse on the way, because some of them have come a long distance.'

4His disciples answered, 'But where in this remote place can anyone get enough bread to feed them?'

5'How many loaves do you have?' Jesus asked.

'Seven,' they replied.

6He told the crowd to sit down on the ground. When he had taken the seven loaves and given thanks, he broke them and gave them to his disciples to distribute to the people, and they did so. 7They had a few small fish as well; he gave thanks for them also and told the disciples to distribute them. 8The people ate and were satisfied. Afterwards the disciples picked up seven basketfuls of broken pieces that were left over. 9About four thousand were present. After he had sent them away, 10he got into the boat with his disciples and went to the region of Dalmanutha.

11The Pharisees came and began to question Jesus. To test him, they asked him for a sign from heaven. 12He sighed deeply and said, 'Why does this generation ask for a sign? Truly I tell you, no sign will be given to it.' 13Then he left them, got back into the boat and crossed to the other side.

The yeast of the Pharisees and Herod

14The disciples had forgotten to bring bread, except for one loaf they had with them in the boat. 15'Be careful,' Jesus warned them. 'Watch out for the yeast of the Pharisees and that of Herod.'

16They discussed this with one another and said, 'It is because we have no bread.'

17Aware of their discussion, Jesus asked them: 'Why are you talking about having no bread? Do you still not see or understand? Are your hearts hardened? [18]Do you have eyes but fail to see, and ears but fail to hear? And don't you remember? [19]When I broke the five loaves for the five thousand, how many basketfuls of pieces did you pick up?'

'Twelve,' they replied.

[20]'And when I broke the seven loaves for the four thousand, how many basketfuls of pieces did you pick up?'

They answered, 'Seven.'

[21]He said to them, 'Do you still not understand?'

Jesus heals a blind man at Bethsaida

[22]They came to Bethsaida, and some people brought a blind man and begged Jesus to touch him. [23]He took the blind man by the hand and led him outside the village. When he had spat on the man's eyes and put his hands on him, Jesus asked, 'Do you see anything?'

[24]He looked up and said, 'I see people; they look like trees walking around.'

[25]Once more Jesus put his hands on the man's eyes. Then his eyes were opened, his sight was restored, and he saw everything clearly. [26]Jesus sent him home, saying, 'Don't even go into[a] the village.'

Peter declares that Jesus is the Messiah

[27]Jesus and his disciples went on to the villages around Caesarea Philippi. On the way he asked them, 'Who do people say I am?'

[28]They replied, 'Some say John the Baptist; others say Elijah; and still others, one of the prophets.'

[29]'But what about you?' he asked. 'Who do you say I am?'
Peter answered, 'You are the Messiah.'

[30]Jesus warned them not to tell anyone about him.

Jesus predicts his death

[31]He then began to teach them that the Son of Man must suffer many things and be rejected by the elders, the chief priests

a 26 Some manuscripts *go and tell anyone in*

THE STORY SO FAR

In the first half of Mark's book, we have seen Jesus amazing people with his power over sickness, nature, sin and death. He does and says some things that have never been seen or heard before. He walks on water, raises the dead, heals the sick, forgives sins, teaches the Scriptures as if he wrote them, and more. This is obviously no ordinary man, and he talks about himself in puzzling ways.

The first half of Mark is really answering the question: **Who is Jesus?** And it seems as if no one really understands. Some are drawn to follow him; some plot to kill him. Sceptics demand signs, but seem to ignore the incredible miracles that Jesus has already done in front of them. Why? Why does he seem so dangerous? Even his closest friends can't see his identity. They look at him and are often baffled and sometimes even terrified.

At the end of chapter 8, Jesus asks his closest followers who people think he is. That's the big question. Is he John the Baptist (see chapter 6, pages 19-20), come back to life? Is he the latest in the line of great prophets, speaking on behalf of God? Or is he the long-awaited Messiah – God's chosen king, the Son of God?

That's the crucial question about Jesus. Is he a great teacher and miracle worker with delusions about himself, or is he truly who he says? Now that we have heard all that is reported about Jesus in the first half, Mark invites us to answer the same question Jesus put to his disciples. **"But what about you? Who do you say I am?"** Peter blurts out his verdict (see verse 29 on the opposite page).

How would you answer the same question after reading the first half of Mark?

WHAT COMES NEXT?

There is a sudden shift in the story after Peter's statement in verse 29. Notice how verse 31 starts: "He then began to teach them…" The question of Jesus' identity has been settled. It's almost as though Lesson 1 – about who Jesus is – has been learned, so he moves on to Lesson 2. And Lesson 2 is all about why Jesus came. It is about his **mission**.

In the second half of his Gospel, Mark shows the tension building and building as Jesus teaches his followers that he is going to die, and explains why. Again and again, Jesus repeats that he will suffer, die and rise again. And the disciples do not understand.

Why does Jesus allow this terrible death to happen? It has to do with God's attitude to our human selfishness. Jesus says we need his rescue because we have a problem with our sinful human hearts. We are not able to make ourselves acceptable to God – we need someone to do that for us.

What emerges in the second half of Mark's Gospel is that Jesus' death on the cross and his coming back to life are the way that we are rescued and made acceptable to God.

In this next section, we will see how Jesus goes to Jerusalem to die. This is Jesus' mission: to suffer, die and rise again so that we can be put right with God and saved from an eternity apart from God, in hell. That's the bottom line. He came to rescue us.

Read on to see how this rescue unfolds, and watch the different reactions that people have to it…

and the teachers of the law, and that he must be killed and after three days rise again. ³²He spoke plainly about this, and Peter took him aside and began to rebuke him.

³³But when Jesus turned and looked at his disciples, he rebuked Peter. 'Get behind me, Satan!' he said. 'You do not have in mind the concerns of God, but merely human concerns.'

The way of the cross

³⁴Then he called the crowd to him along with his disciples and said: 'Whoever wants to be my disciple must deny themselves and take up their cross and follow me. ³⁵For whoever wants to save their life[b] will lose it, but whoever loses their life for me and for the gospel will save it. ³⁶What good is it for someone to gain the whole world, yet forfeit their soul? ³⁷Or what can anyone give in exchange for their soul? ³⁸If anyone is ashamed of me and my words in this adulterous and sinful generation, the Son of Man will be ashamed of them when he comes in his Father's glory with the holy angels.'

9 And he said to them, 'Truly I tell you, some who are standing here will not taste death before they see that the kingdom of God has come with power.'

The transfiguration

²After six days Jesus took Peter, James and John with him and led them up a high mountain, where they were all alone. There he was transfigured before them. ³His clothes became dazzling white, whiter than anyone in the world could bleach them. ⁴And there appeared before them Elijah and Moses, who were talking with Jesus.

⁵Peter said to Jesus, 'Rabbi, it is good for us to be here. Let us put up three shelters – one for you, one for Moses and one for Elijah.' ⁶(He did not know what to say, they were so frightened.)

⁷Then a cloud appeared and covered them, and a voice came from the cloud: 'This is my Son, whom I love. Listen to him!'

b 35 The Greek word means either *life* or *soul*; also in verses 36 and 37.

⁸Suddenly, when they looked around, they no longer saw anyone with them except Jesus.

⁹As they were coming down the mountain, Jesus gave them orders not to tell anyone what they had seen until the Son of Man had risen from the dead. ¹⁰They kept the matter to themselves, discussing what 'rising from the dead' meant.

¹¹And they asked him, 'Why do the teachers of the law say that Elijah must come first?'

¹²Jesus replied, 'To be sure, Elijah does come first, and restores all things. Why then is it written that the Son of Man must suffer much and be rejected? ¹³But I tell you, Elijah has come, and they have done to him everything they wished, just as it is written about him.'

Jesus heals a boy possessed by an impure spirit

¹⁴When they came to the other disciples, they saw a large crowd around them and the teachers of the law arguing with them. ¹⁵As soon as all the people saw Jesus, they were overwhelmed with wonder and ran to greet him.

¹⁶'What are you arguing with them about?' he asked.

¹⁷A man in the crowd answered, 'Teacher, I brought you my son, who is possessed by a spirit that has robbed him of speech. ¹⁸Whenever it seizes him, it throws him to the ground. He foams at the mouth, gnashes his teeth and becomes rigid. I asked your disciples to drive out the spirit, but they could not.'

¹⁹'You unbelieving generation,' Jesus replied, 'how long shall I stay with you? How long shall I put up with you? Bring the boy to me.'

²⁰So they brought him. When the spirit saw Jesus, it immediately threw the boy into a convulsion. He fell to the ground and rolled around, foaming at the mouth.

²¹Jesus asked the boy's father, 'How long has he been like this?'

'From childhood,' he answered. ²²'It has often thrown him

into fire or water to kill him. But if you can do anything, take pity on us and help us.'

23 ' "If you can"?' said Jesus. 'Everything is possible for one who believes.'

24 Immediately the boy's father exclaimed, 'I do believe; help me overcome my unbelief!'

25 When Jesus saw that a crowd was running to the scene, he rebuked the impure spirit. 'You deaf and mute spirit,' he said, 'I command you, come out of him and never enter him again.'

26 The spirit shrieked, convulsed him violently and came out. The boy looked so much like a corpse that many said, 'He's dead.' 27 But Jesus took him by the hand and lifted him to his feet, and he stood up.

28 After Jesus had gone indoors, his disciples asked him privately, 'Why couldn't we drive it out?'

29 He replied, 'This kind can come out only by prayer.a'

Jesus predicts his death a second time

30 They left that place and passed through Galilee. Jesus did not want anyone to know where they were, 31 because he was teaching his disciples. He said to them, 'The Son of Man is going to be delivered into the hands of men. They will kill him, and after three days he will rise.' 32 But they did not understand what he meant and were afraid to ask him about it.

33 They came to Capernaum. When he was in the house, he asked them, 'What were you arguing about on the road?' 34 But they kept quiet because on the way they had argued about who was the greatest.

35 Sitting down, Jesus called the Twelve and said, 'Anyone who wants to be first must be the very last, and the servant of all.'

36 He took a little child whom he placed among them. Taking the child in his arms, he said to them, 37 'Whoever welcomes one of these little children in my name welcomes me; and whoever welcomes me does not welcome me but the one who sent me.'

a 29 Some manuscripts *prayer and fasting*

Whoever is not against us is for us

38 'Teacher,' said John, 'we saw someone driving out demons in your name and we told him to stop, because he was not one of us.'

39 'Do not stop him,' Jesus said. 'For no one who does a miracle in my name can in the next moment say anything bad about me, 40 for whoever is not against us is for us. 41 Truly I tell you, anyone who gives you a cup of water in my name because you belong to the Messiah will certainly not lose their reward.

Causing to stumble

42 'If anyone causes one of these little ones – those who believe in me – to stumble, it would be better for them if a large millstone were hung round their neck and they were thrown into the sea. 43 If your hand causes you to stumble, cut it off. It is better for you to enter life maimed than with two hands to go into hell, where the fire never goes out. [44]b 45 And if your foot causes you to stumble, cut it off. It is better for you to enter life crippled than to have two feet and be thrown into hell. [46]b 47 And if your eye causes you to stumble, pluck it out. It is better for you to enter the kingdom of God with one eye than to have two eyes and be thrown into hell, 48 where

> '"the worms that eat them do not die,
>   and the fire is not quenched."c

49 Everyone will be salted with fire.

50 'Salt is good, but if it loses its saltiness, how can you make it salty again? Have salt among yourselves, and be at peace with each other.'

b 44,46 Some manuscripts include here the words of verse 48.
c 48 Isaiah 66:24

Divorce

10 Jesus then left that place and went into the region of Judea and across the Jordan. Again crowds of people came to him, and as was his custom, he taught them.

2 Some Pharisees came and tested him by asking, 'Is it lawful for a man to divorce his wife?'

3 'What did Moses command you?' he replied.

4 They said, 'Moses permitted a man to write a certificate of divorce and send her away.'

5 'It was because your hearts were hard that Moses wrote you this law,' Jesus replied. 6 'But at the beginning of creation God "made them male and female".[a] 7 "For this reason a man will leave his father and mother and be united to his wife,[b] 8 and the two will become one flesh."[c] So they are no longer two, but one flesh. 9 Therefore what God has joined together, let no one separate.'

10 When they were in the house again, the disciples asked Jesus about this. 11 He answered, 'Anyone who divorces his wife and marries another woman commits adultery against her. 12 And if she divorces her husband and marries another man, she commits adultery.'

The little children and Jesus

13 People were bringing little children to Jesus for him to place his hands on them, but the disciples rebuked them. 14 When Jesus saw this, he was indignant. He said to them, 'Let the little children come to me, and do not hinder them, for the kingdom of God belongs to such as these. 15 Truly I tell you, anyone who will not receive the kingdom of God like a little child will never enter it.' 16 And he took the children in his arms, placed his hands on them and blessed them.

a 6 Gen. 1:27
b 7 Some early manuscripts do not have *and be united to his wife*.
c 8 Gen. 2:24

The rich and the kingdom of God

¹⁷As Jesus started on his way, a man ran up to him and fell on his knees before him. 'Good teacher,' he asked, 'what must I do to inherit eternal life?'

¹⁸'Why do you call me good?' Jesus answered. 'No one is good – except God alone. ¹⁹You know the commandments: "You shall not murder, you shall not commit adultery, you shall not steal, you shall not give false testimony, you shall not defraud, honour your father and mother."^d'

²⁰'Teacher,' he declared, 'all these I have kept since I was a boy.'

²¹Jesus looked at him and loved him. 'One thing you lack,' he said. 'Go, sell everything you have and give to the poor, and you will have treasure in heaven. Then come, follow me.'

²²At this the man's face fell. He went away sad, because he had great wealth.

²³Jesus looked round and said to his disciples, 'How hard it is for the rich to enter the kingdom of God!'

²⁴The disciples were amazed at his words. But Jesus said again, 'Children, how hard it is^e to enter the kingdom of God! ²⁵It is easier for a camel to go through the eye of a needle than for someone who is rich to enter the kingdom of God.'

²⁶The disciples were even more amazed, and said to each other, 'Who then can be saved?'

²⁷Jesus looked at them and said, 'With man this is impossible, but not with God; all things are possible with God.'

²⁸Then Peter spoke up, 'We have left everything to follow you!'

²⁹'Truly I tell you,' Jesus replied, 'no one who has left home or brothers or sisters or mother or father or children or fields for me and the gospel ³⁰will fail to receive a hundred times as much in this present age: homes, brothers, sisters, mothers, children and fields – along with persecutions – and in the age to come eternal life. ³¹But many who are first will be last, and the last first.'

d 19 Exodus 20:12-16; Deut. 5:16-20
e 24 Some manuscripts *is for those who trust in riches*

Jesus predicts his death a third time

32 They were on their way up to Jerusalem, with Jesus leading the way, and the disciples were astonished, while those who followed were afraid. Again he took the Twelve aside and told them what was going to happen to him. 33 'We are going up to Jerusalem,' he said, 'and the Son of Man will be delivered over to the chief priests and the teachers of the law. They will condemn him to death and will hand him over to the Gentiles, 34 who will mock him and spit on him, flog him and kill him. Three days later he will rise.'

The request of James and John

35 Then James and John, the sons of Zebedee, came to him. 'Teacher,' they said, 'we want you to do for us whatever we ask.'

36 'What do you want me to do for you?' he asked.

37 They replied, 'Let one of us sit at your right and the other at your left in your glory.'

38 'You don't know what you are asking,' Jesus said. 'Can you drink the cup I drink or be baptised with the baptism I am baptised with?'

39 'We can,' they answered.

Jesus said to them, 'You will drink the cup I drink and be baptised with the baptism I am baptised with, 40 but to sit at my right or left is not for me to grant. These places belong to those for whom they have been prepared.'

41 When the ten heard about this, they became indignant with James and John. 42 Jesus called them together and said, 'You know that those who are regarded as rulers of the Gentiles lord it over them, and their high officials exercise authority over them. 43 Not so with you. Instead, whoever wants to become great among you must be your servant, 44 and whoever wants to be first must be slave of all. 45 For even the Son of Man did not come to be served, but to serve, and to give his life as a ransom for many.'

Blind Bartimaeus receives his sight

⁴⁶Then they came to Jericho. As Jesus and his disciples, together with a large crowd, were leaving the city, a blind man, Bartimaeus (which means 'son of Timaeus'), was sitting by the roadside begging. ⁴⁷When he heard that it was Jesus of Nazareth, he began to shout, 'Jesus, Son of David, have mercy on me!'

⁴⁸Many rebuked him and told him to be quiet, but he shouted all the more, 'Son of David, have mercy on me!'

⁴⁹Jesus stopped and said, 'Call him.'

So they called to the blind man, 'Cheer up! On your feet! He's calling you.' ⁵⁰Throwing his cloak aside, he jumped to his feet and came to Jesus.

⁵¹'What do you want me to do for you?' Jesus asked him.

The blind man said, 'Rabbi, I want to see.'

⁵²'Go,' said Jesus, 'your faith has healed you.' Immediately he received his sight and followed Jesus along the road.

Jesus comes to Jerusalem as king

11 As they approached Jerusalem and came to Bethphage and Bethany at the Mount of Olives, Jesus sent two of his disciples, ²saying to them, 'Go to the village ahead of you, and just as you enter it, you will find a colt tied there, which no one has ever ridden. Untie it and bring it here. ³If anyone asks you, "Why are you doing this?" say, "The Lord needs it and will send it back here shortly."'

⁴They went and found a colt outside in the street, tied at a doorway. As they untied it, ⁵some people standing there asked, 'What are you doing, untying that colt?' ⁶They answered as Jesus had told them to, and the people let them go. ⁷When they brought the colt to Jesus and threw their cloaks over it, he sat on it. ⁸Many people spread their cloaks on the road, while others spread branches they had cut in the fields. ⁹Those who went ahead and those who followed shouted,

> 'Hosanna![a]'
>
> 'Blessed is he who comes in the name of the Lord!'[b]
>
> 10 'Blessed is the coming kingdom of our father David!'
>
> 'Hosanna in the highest heaven!'

11 Jesus entered Jerusalem and went into the temple courts. He looked around at everything, but since it was already late, he went out to Bethany with the Twelve.

Jesus curses a fig-tree and clears the temple courts

12 The next day as they were leaving Bethany, Jesus was hungry. 13 Seeing in the distance a fig-tree in leaf, he went to find out if it had any fruit. When he reached it, he found nothing but leaves, because it was not the season for figs. 14 Then he said to the tree, 'May no one ever eat fruit from you again.' And his disciples heard him say it.

15 On reaching Jerusalem, Jesus entered the temple courts and began driving out those who were buying and selling there. He overturned the tables of the money-changers and the benches of those selling doves, 16 and would not allow anyone to carry merchandise through the temple courts. 17 And as he taught them, he said, 'Is it not written: "My house will be called a house of prayer for all nations"[c]? But you have made it "a den of robbers".[d]'

18 The chief priests and the teachers of the law heard this and began looking for a way to kill him, for they feared him, because the whole crowd was amazed at his teaching.

19 When evening came, Jesus and his disciples[e] went out of the city.

20 In the morning, as they went along, they saw the fig-tree withered from the roots. 21 Peter remembered and said to Jesus, 'Rabbi, look! The fig-tree you cursed has withered!'

---

a 9 A Hebrew expression meaning 'Save!' which became an exclamation of praise; also in verse 10
b 9 Psalm 118:25,26
c 17 Isaiah 56:7
d 17 Jer. 7:11
e 19 Some early manuscripts came, *Jesus*

²²'Have faith in God,' Jesus answered. ²³'Truly[f] I tell you, if anyone says to this mountain, "Go, throw yourself into the sea," and does not doubt in their heart but believes that what they say will happen, it will be done for them. ²⁴Therefore I tell you, whatever you ask for in prayer, believe that you have received it, and it will be yours. ²⁵And when you stand praying, if you hold anything against anyone, forgive them, so that your Father in heaven may forgive you your sins.' [26][g]

The authority of Jesus questioned

²⁷They arrived again in Jerusalem, and while Jesus was walking in the temple courts, the chief priests, the teachers of the law and the elders came to him. ²⁸'By what authority are you doing these things?' they asked. 'And who gave you authority to do this?'

²⁹Jesus replied, 'I will ask you one question. Answer me, and I will tell you by what authority I am doing these things. ³⁰John's baptism – was it from heaven, or of human origin? Tell me!'

³¹They discussed it among themselves and said, 'If we say, "From heaven," he will ask, "Then why didn't you believe him?" ³²But if we say, "Of human origin" . . .' (They feared the people, for everyone held that John really was a prophet.)

³³So they answered Jesus, 'We don't know.'

Jesus said, 'Neither will I tell you by what authority I am doing these things.'

The parable of the tenants

12 Jesus then began to speak to them in parables: 'A man planted a vineyard. He put a wall round it, dug a pit for the winepress and built a watchtower. Then he rented the vineyard to some farmers and moved to another place. ²At harvest time he sent a servant to the tenants to collect from them some of the fruit of the vineyard. ³But they seized him, beat him and sent him away empty-handed. ⁴Then he sent another servant to them; they struck this man on the head and treated him

f 22,23 Some early manuscripts 'If you have faith in God,' Jesus answered, ²³'truly
g 26 Some manuscripts include here words similar to Matt. 6:15.

shamefully. ⁵He sent still another, and that one they killed. He sent many others; some of them they beat, others they killed.

⁶'He had one left to send, a son, whom he loved. He sent him last of all, saying, "They will respect my son."

⁷'But the tenants said to one another, "This is the heir. Come, let's kill him, and the inheritance will be ours." ⁸So they took him and killed him, and threw him out of the vineyard.

⁹'What then will the owner of the vineyard do? He will come and kill those tenants and give the vineyard to others. ¹⁰Haven't you read this passage of Scripture:

> ' *"The stone the builders rejected*
> *has become the cornerstone;*
> ¹¹ *the Lord has done this,*
> *and it is marvellous in our eyes"*ᵃ?'

¹²Then the chief priests, the teachers of the law and the elders looked for a way to arrest him because they knew he had spoken the parable against them. But they were afraid of the crowd; so they left him and went away.

Paying the poll-tax to Caesar

¹³Later they sent some of the Pharisees and Herodians to Jesus to catch him in his words. ¹⁴They came to him and said, 'Teacher, we know that you are a man of integrity. You aren't swayed by others, because you pay no attention to who they are; but you teach the way of God in accordance with the truth. Is it right to pay the poll-taxᵇ to Caesar or not? ¹⁵Should we pay or shouldn't we?'

But Jesus knew their hypocrisy. 'Why are you trying to trap me?' he asked. 'Bring me a denarius and let me look at it.' ¹⁶They brought the coin, and he asked them, 'Whose image is this? And whose inscription?'

'Caesar's,' they replied.

¹⁷Then Jesus said to them, 'Give back to Caesar what is Caesar's and to God what is God's.'

And they were amazed at him.

a 11 Psalm 118:22,23
b 14 A special tax levied on subject peoples, not on Roman citizens

Marriage at the resurrection

18 Then the Sadducees, who say there is no resurrection, came to him with a question. 19 'Teacher,' they said, 'Moses wrote for us that if a man's brother dies and leaves a wife but no children, the man must marry the widow and raise up offspring for his brother. 20 Now there were seven brothers. The first one married and died without leaving any children. 21 The second one married the widow, but he also died, leaving no child. It was the same with the third. 22 In fact, none of the seven left any children. Last of all, the woman died too. 23 At the resurrection^c whose wife will she be, since the seven were married to her?'

24 Jesus replied, 'Are you not in error because you do not know the Scriptures or the power of God? 25 When the dead rise, they will neither marry nor be given in marriage; they will be like the angels in heaven. 26 Now about the dead rising – have you not read in the Book of Moses, in the account of the burning bush, how God said to him, "I am the God of Abraham, the God of Isaac, and the God of Jacob"^{d}? 27 He is not the God of the dead, but of the living. You are badly mistaken!'

The greatest commandment

28 One of the teachers of the law came and heard them debating. Noticing that Jesus had given them a good answer, he asked him, 'Of all the commandments, which is the most important?'

29 'The most important one,' answered Jesus, 'is this: "Hear, O Israel: the Lord our God, the Lord is one.^{e} 30 Love the Lord your God with all your heart and with all your soul and with all your mind and with all your strength."^{f} 31 The second is this: "Love your neighbour as yourself."^{g} There is no commandment greater than these.'

32 'Well said, teacher,' the man replied. 'You are right in saying that God is one and there is no other but him. 33 To love

c 23 Some manuscripts *resurrection, when people rise from the dead,*
d 26 Exodus 3:6
e 29 Or *the Lord our God is one Lord*
f 30 Deut. 6:4,5
g 31 Lev. 19:18

him with all your heart, with all your understanding and with all your strength, and to love your neighbour as yourself is more important than all burnt offerings and sacrifices.'

³⁴When Jesus saw that he had answered wisely, he said to him, 'You are not far from the kingdom of God.' And from then on no one dared ask him any more questions.

Whose son is the Messiah?

³⁵While Jesus was teaching in the temple courts, he asked, 'Why do the teachers of the law say that the Messiah is the son of David? ³⁶David himself, speaking by the Holy Spirit, declared:

> ' "The Lord said to my Lord:
> 'Sit at my right hand
> until I put your enemies
> under your feet.' " ʰ

³⁷David himself calls him "Lord". How then can he be his son?'

The large crowd listened to him with delight.

Warning against the teachers of the law

³⁸As he taught, Jesus said, 'Watch out for the teachers of the law. They like to walk around in flowing robes and be greeted with respect in the market-places, ³⁹and have the most important seats in the synagogues and the places of honour at banquets. ⁴⁰They devour widows' houses and for a show make lengthy prayers. These men will be punished most severely.'

The widow's offering

⁴¹Jesus sat down opposite the place where the offerings were put and watched the crowd putting their money into the temple treasury. Many rich people threw in large amounts. ⁴²But a poor widow came and put in two very small copper coins, worth only a few pence.

⁴³Calling his disciples to him, Jesus said, 'Truly I tell you, this

h 36 Psalm 110:1

poor widow has put more into the treasury than all the others. [44]They all gave out of their wealth; but she, out of her poverty, put in everything – all she had to live on.'

The destruction of the temple and signs of the end times

13 As Jesus was leaving the temple, one of his disciples said to him, 'Look, Teacher! What massive stones! What magnificent buildings!'

[2]'Do you see all these great buildings?' replied Jesus. 'Not one stone here will be left on another; every one will be thrown down.'

[3]As Jesus was sitting on the Mount of Olives opposite the temple, Peter, James, John and Andrew asked him privately, [4]'Tell us, when will these things happen? And what will be the sign that they are all about to be fulfilled?'

[5]Jesus said to them: 'Watch out that no one deceives you. [6]Many will come in my name, claiming, "I am he," and will deceive many. [7]When you hear of wars and rumours of wars, do not be alarmed. Such things must happen, but the end is still to come. [8]Nation will rise against nation, and kingdom against kingdom. There will be earthquakes in various places, and famines. These are the beginning of birth-pains.

[9]'You must be on your guard. You will be handed over to the local councils and flogged in the synagogues. On account of me you will stand before governors and kings as witnesses to them. [10]And the gospel must first be preached to all nations. [11]Whenever you are arrested and brought to trial, do not worry beforehand about what to say. Just say whatever is given you at the time, for it is not you speaking, but the Holy Spirit.

[12]'Brother will betray brother to death, and a father his child. Children will rebel against their parents and have them put to death. [13]Everyone will hate you because of me, but the one who stands firm to the end will be saved.

[14]'When you see "the abomination that causes desolation"[a] standing where it[b] does not belong – let the reader understand – then let those who are in Judea flee to the mountains.

a 14 Daniel 9:27; 11:31; 12:11
b 14 Or he

42

¹⁵ Let no one on the housetop go down or enter the house to take anything out. ¹⁶ Let no one in the field go back to get their cloak. ¹⁷ How dreadful it will be in those days for pregnant women and nursing mothers! ¹⁸ Pray that this will not take place in winter, ¹⁹ because those will be days of distress unequalled from the beginning, when God created the world, until now – and never to be equalled again.

²⁰ 'If the Lord had not cut short those days, no one would survive. But for the sake of the elect, whom he has chosen, he has shortened them. ²¹ At that time if anyone says to you, "Look, here is the Messiah!" or, "Look, there he is!" do not believe it. ²² For false messiahs and false prophets will appear and perform signs and wonders to deceive, if possible, even the elect. ²³ So be on your guard; I have told you everything in advance.

²⁴ 'But in those days, following that distress,

> ' *"the sun will be darkened,*
> *and the moon will not give its light;*
> ²⁵ *the stars will fall from the sky,*
> *and the heavenly bodies will be shaken."* c

²⁶ 'At that time people will see the Son of Man coming in clouds with great power and glory. ²⁷ And he will send his angels and gather his elect from the four winds, from the ends of the earth to the ends of the heavens.

²⁸ 'Now learn this lesson from the fig-tree: As soon as its twigs get tender and its leaves come out, you know that summer is near. ²⁹ Even so, when you see these things happening, you know that it d is near, right at the door. ³⁰ Truly I tell you, this generation will certainly not pass away until all these things have happened. ³¹ Heaven and earth will pass away, but my words will never pass away.

The day and hour unknown

³² 'But about that day or hour no one knows, not even the

c 25 Isaiah 13:10; 34:4
d 29 Or he

angels in heaven, nor the Son, but only the Father. ³³Be on guard! Be alert[e]! You do not know when that time will come. ³⁴It's like a man going away: he leaves his house and puts his servants in charge, each with their assigned task, and tells the one at the door to keep watch.

³⁵'Therefore keep watch because you do not know when the owner of the house will come back – whether in the evening, or at midnight, or when the cock crows, or at dawn. ³⁶If he comes suddenly, do not let him find you sleeping. ³⁷What I say to you, I say to everyone: "Watch!"'

Jesus anointed at Bethany

14 Now the Passover and the Festival of Unleavened Bread were only two days away, and the chief priests and the teachers of the law were scheming to arrest Jesus secretly and kill him. ²'But not during the festival,' they said, 'or the people may riot.'

³While he was in Bethany, reclining at the table in the home of Simon the Leper, a woman came with an alabaster jar of very expensive perfume, made of pure nard. She broke the jar and poured the perfume on his head.

⁴Some of those present were saying indignantly to one another, 'Why this waste of perfume? ⁵It could have been sold for more than a year's wages[a] and the money given to the poor.' And they rebuked her harshly.

⁶'Leave her alone,' said Jesus. 'Why are you bothering her? She has done a beautiful thing to me. ⁷The poor you will always have with you,[b] and you can help them any time you want. But you will not always have me. ⁸She did what she could. She poured perfume on my body beforehand to prepare for my burial. ⁹Truly I tell you, wherever the gospel is preached throughout the world, what she has done will also be told, in memory of her.'

¹⁰Then Judas Iscariot, one of the Twelve, went to the chief priests to betray Jesus to them. ¹¹They were delighted to hear

e 33 Some manuscripts *alert and pray*
a 5 Greek *than three hundred denarii*
b 7 See Deut. 15:11.

this and promised to give him money. So he watched for an opportunity to hand him over.

The Last Supper

¹²On the first day of the Festival of Unleavened Bread, when it was customary to sacrifice the Passover lamb, Jesus' disciples asked him, 'Where do you want us to go and make preparations for you to eat the Passover?'

¹³So he sent two of his disciples, telling them, 'Go into the city, and a man carrying a jar of water will meet you. Follow him. ¹⁴Say to the owner of the house he enters, "The Teacher asks: where is my guest room, where I may eat the Passover with my disciples?" ¹⁵He will show you a large room upstairs, furnished and ready. Make preparations for us there.'

¹⁶The disciples left, went into the city and found things just as Jesus had told them. So they prepared the Passover.

¹⁷When evening came, Jesus arrived with the Twelve. ¹⁸While they were reclining at the table eating, he said, 'Truly I tell you, one of you will betray me – one who is eating with me.'

¹⁹They were saddened, and one by one they said to him, 'Surely you don't mean me?'

²⁰'It is one of the Twelve,' he replied, 'one who dips bread into the bowl with me. ²¹The Son of Man will go just as it is written about him. But woe to that man who betrays the Son of Man! It would be better for him if he had not been born.'

²²While they were eating, Jesus took bread, and when he had given thanks, he broke it and gave it to his disciples, saying, 'Take it; this is my body.'

²³Then he took a cup, and when he had given thanks, he gave it to them, and they all drank from it.

²⁴'This is my blood of the^c covenant, which is poured out for many,' he said to them. ²⁵'Truly I tell you, I will not drink again from the fruit of the vine until that day when I drink it new in the kingdom of God.'

²⁶When they had sung a hymn, they went out to the Mount of Olives.

c 24 Some manuscripts *the new*

Jesus predicts Peter's denial

27 'You will all fall away,' Jesus told them, 'for it is written:

> '"I will strike the shepherd,
>   and the sheep will be scattered."d

28 But after I have risen, I will go ahead of you into Galilee.'

29 Peter declared, 'Even if all fall away, I will not.'

30 'Truly I tell you,' Jesus answered, 'today – yes, tonight – before the cock crows twicee you yourself will disown me three times.'

31 But Peter insisted emphatically, 'Even if I have to die with you, I will never disown you.' And all the others said the same.

Gethsemane

32 They went to a place called Gethsemane, and Jesus said to his disciples, 'Sit here while I pray.' 33 He took Peter, James and John along with him, and he began to be deeply distressed and troubled. 34 'My soul is overwhelmed with sorrow to the point of death,' he said to them. 'Stay here and keep watch.'

35 Going a little farther, he fell to the ground and prayed that if possible the hour might pass from him. 36 'Abba,f Father,' he said, 'everything is possible for you. Take this cup from me. Yet not what I will, but what you will.'

37 Then he returned to his disciples and found them sleeping. 'Simon,' he said to Peter, 'are you asleep? Couldn't you keep watch for one hour? 38 Watch and pray so that you will not fall into temptation. The spirit is willing, but the flesh is weak.'

39 Once more he went away and prayed the same thing. 40 When he came back, he again found them sleeping, because their eyes were heavy. They did not know what to say to him.

41 Returning the third time, he said to them, 'Are you still sleeping and resting? Enough! The hour has come. Look, the Son of Man is delivered into the hands of sinners. 42 Rise! Let us go! Here comes my betrayer!'

d 27 Zech. 13:7
e 30 Some early manuscripts do not have *twice*.
f 36 Aramaic for *father*

Jesus arrested

⁴³Just as he was speaking, Judas, one of the Twelve, appeared. With him was a crowd armed with swords and clubs, sent from the chief priests, the teachers of the law, and the elders.

⁴⁴Now the betrayer had arranged a signal with them: 'The one I kiss is the man; arrest him and lead him away under guard.' ⁴⁵Going at once to Jesus, Judas said, 'Rabbi!' and kissed him. ⁴⁶The men seized Jesus and arrested him. ⁴⁷Then one of those standing near drew his sword and struck the servant of the high priest, cutting off his ear.

⁴⁸'Am I leading a rebellion,' said Jesus, 'that you have come out with swords and clubs to capture me? ⁴⁹Every day I was with you, teaching in the temple courts, and you did not arrest me. But the Scriptures must be fulfilled.' ⁵⁰Then everyone deserted him and fled.

⁵¹A young man, wearing nothing but a linen garment, was following Jesus. When they seized him, ⁵²he fled naked, leaving his garment behind.

Jesus before the Sanhedrin

⁵³They took Jesus to the high priest, and all the chief priests, the elders and the teachers of the law came together. ⁵⁴Peter followed him at a distance, right into the courtyard of the high priest. There he sat with the guards and warmed himself at the fire.

⁵⁵The chief priests and the whole Sanhedrin were looking for evidence against Jesus so that they could put him to death, but they did not find any. ⁵⁶Many testified falsely against him, but their statements did not agree.

⁵⁷Then some stood up and gave this false testimony against him: ⁵⁸'We heard him say, "I will destroy this temple made with human hands and in three days will build another, not made with hands."' ⁵⁹Yet even then their testimony did not agree.

⁶⁰Then the high priest stood up before them and asked Jesus, 'Are you not going to answer? What is this testimony that these

men are bringing against you?' 61 But Jesus remained silent and gave no answer.

Again the high priest asked him, 'Are you the Messiah, the Son of the Blessed One?'

62 'I am,' said Jesus. 'And you will see the Son of Man sitting at the right hand of the Mighty One and coming on the clouds of heaven.'

63 The high priest tore his clothes. 'Why do we need any more witnesses?' he asked. 64 'You have heard the blasphemy. What do you think?'

They all condemned him as worthy of death. 65 Then some began to spit at him; they blindfolded him, struck him with their fists, and said, 'Prophesy!' And the guards took him and beat him.

Peter disowns Jesus

66 While Peter was below in the courtyard, one of the servant-girls of the high priest came by. 67 When she saw Peter warming himself, she looked closely at him.

'You also were with that Nazarene, Jesus,' she said.

68 But he denied it. 'I don't know or understand what you're talking about,' he said, and went out into the entrance.g

69 When the servant-girl saw him there, she said again to those standing round them, 'This fellow is one of them.' 70 Again he denied it.

After a little while, those standing near said to Peter, 'Surely you are one of them, for you are a Galilean.'

71 He began to call down curses, and he swore to them, 'I don't know this man you're talking about.'

72 Immediately the cock crowed the second time.h Then Peter remembered the word Jesus had spoken to him: 'Before the cock crows twicei you will disown me three times.' And he broke down and wept.

g 68 Some early manuscripts *entrance and the cock crowed*
h 72 Some early manuscripts do not have *the second time*.
i 72 Some early manuscripts do not have *twice*.

Jesus before Pilate

15 Very early in the morning, the chief priests, with the elders, the teachers of the law and the whole Sanhedrin, made their plans. So they bound Jesus, led him away and handed him over to Pilate.

² 'Are you the king of the Jews?' asked Pilate.

'You have said so,' Jesus replied.

³ The chief priests accused him of many things. ⁴ So again Pilate asked him, 'Aren't you going to answer? See how many things they are accusing you of.'

⁵ But Jesus still made no reply, and Pilate was amazed.

⁶ Now it was the custom at the festival to release a prisoner whom the people requested. ⁷ A man called Barabbas was in prison with the rebels who had committed murder in the uprising. ⁸ The crowd came up and asked Pilate to do for them what he usually did.

⁹ 'Do you want me to release to you the king of the Jews?' asked Pilate, ¹⁰ knowing it was out of self-interest that the chief priests had handed Jesus over to him. ¹¹ But the chief priests stirred up the crowd to get Pilate to release Barabbas instead.

¹² 'What shall I do, then, with the one you call the king of the Jews?' Pilate asked them.

¹³ 'Crucify him!' they shouted.

¹⁴ 'Why? What crime has he committed?' asked Pilate.

But they shouted all the louder, 'Crucify him!'

¹⁵ Wanting to satisfy the crowd, Pilate released Barabbas to them. He had Jesus flogged, and handed him over to be crucified.

The soldiers mock Jesus

¹⁶ The soldiers led Jesus away into the palace (that is, the Praetorium) and called together the whole company of soldiers. ¹⁷ They put a purple robe on him, then twisted together a crown of thorns and set it on him. ¹⁸ And they began to call out to him, 'Hail, king of the Jews!' ¹⁹ Again and again they struck him on the head with a staff and spat on him. Falling on their

knees, they paid homage to him. ²⁰And when they had mocked him, they took off the purple robe and put his own clothes on him. Then they led him out to crucify him.

The crucifixion of Jesus

²¹A certain man from Cyrene, Simon, the father of Alexander and Rufus, was passing by on his way in from the country, and they forced him to carry the cross. ²²They brought Jesus to the place called Golgotha (which means 'the place of the skull'). ²³Then they offered him wine mixed with myrrh, but he did not take it. ²⁴And they crucified him. Dividing up his clothes, they cast lots to see what each would get.

²⁵It was nine in the morning when they crucified him. ²⁶The written notice of the charge against him read: THE KING OF THE JEWS.

²⁷They crucified two rebels with him, one on his right and one on his left. [28]a ²⁹Those who passed by hurled insults at him, shaking their heads and saying, 'So! You who are going to destroy the temple and build it in three days, ³⁰come down from the cross and save yourself!' ³¹In the same way the chief priests and the teachers of the law mocked him among themselves. 'He saved others,' they said, 'but he can't save himself! ³²Let this Messiah, this king of Israel, come down now from the cross, that we may see and believe.' Those crucified with him also heaped insults on him.

The death of Jesus

³³At noon, darkness came over the whole land until three in the afternoon. ³⁴And at three in the afternoon Jesus cried out in a loud voice, *'Eloi, Eloi, lema sabachthani?'* (which means 'My God, my God, why have you forsaken me?').b

³⁵When some of those standing near heard this, they said, 'Listen, he's calling Elijah.'

³⁶Someone ran, filled a sponge with wine vinegar, put it on a staff, and offered it to Jesus to drink. 'Now leave him alone. Let's see if Elijah comes to take him down,' he said.

a 28 Some manuscripts include here words similar to Luke 22:37.
b 34 Psalm 22:1

37 With a loud cry, Jesus breathed his last.

38 The curtain of the temple was torn in two from top to bottom. 39 And when the centurion, who stood there in front of Jesus, saw how he died,ᶜ he said, 'Surely this man was the Son of God!'

40 Some women were watching from a distance. Among them were Mary Magdalene, Mary the mother of James the younger and of Joseph,ᵈ and Salome. 41 In Galilee these women had followed him and cared for his needs. Many other women who had come up with him to Jerusalem were also there.

The burial of Jesus

42 It was Preparation Day (that is, the day before the Sabbath). So as evening approached, 43 Joseph of Arimathea, a prominent member of the Council, who was himself waiting for the kingdom of God, went boldly to Pilate and asked for Jesus' body. 44 Pilate was surprised to hear that he was already dead. Summoning the centurion, he asked him if Jesus had already died. 45 When he learned from the centurion that it was so, he gave the body to Joseph. 46 So Joseph bought some linen cloth, took down the body, wrapped it in the linen, and placed it in a tomb cut out of rock. Then he rolled a stone against the entrance of the tomb. 47 Mary Magdalene and Mary the mother of Joseph saw where he was laid.

Jesus has risen

16 When the Sabbath was over, Mary Magdalene, Mary the mother of James, and Salome bought spices so that they might go to anoint Jesus' body. 2 Very early on the first day of the week, just after sunrise, they were on their way to the tomb 3 and they asked each other, 'Who will roll the stone away from the entrance of the tomb?'

4 But when they looked up, they saw that the stone, which was very large, had been rolled away. 5 As they entered the tomb, they saw a young man dressed in a white robe sitting on the right side, and they were alarmed.

c 39 Some manuscripts *saw that he died with such a cry*
d 40 Greek *Joses*, a variant of *Joseph*; also in verse 47

⁶'Don't be alarmed,' he said. 'You are looking for Jesus the Nazarene, who was crucified. He has risen! He is not here. See the place where they laid him. ⁷But go, tell his disciples and Peter, "He is going ahead of you into Galilee. There you will see him, just as he told you."'

⁸Trembling and bewildered, the women went out and fled from the tomb. They said nothing to anyone, because they were afraid.ᵃ

[The earliest manuscripts and some other ancient witnesses do not have verses 9 – 20.]

⁹When Jesus rose early on the first day of the week, he appeared first to Mary Magdalene, out of whom he had driven seven demons. ¹⁰She went and told those who had been with him and who were mourning and weeping. ¹¹When they heard that Jesus was alive and that she had seen him, they did not believe it.

¹²Afterwards Jesus appeared in a different form to two of them while they were walking in the country. ¹³These returned and reported it to the rest; but they did not believe them either.

¹⁴Later Jesus appeared to the Eleven as they were eating; he rebuked them for their lack of faith and their stubborn refusal to believe those who had seen him after he had risen.

¹⁵He said to them, 'Go into all the world and preach the gospel to all creation. ¹⁶Whoever believes and is baptised will be saved, but whoever does not believe will be condemned. ¹⁷And these signs will accompany those who believe: in my name they will drive out demons; they will speak in new tongues; ¹⁸they will pick up snakes with their hands; and when they drink deadly

a 8 Some manuscripts have the following ending between verses 8 and 9, and one manuscript has it after verse 8 (omitting verses 9-20): *Then they quickly reported all these instructions to those around Peter. After this, Jesus himself also sent out through them from east to west the sacred and imperishable proclamation of eternal salvation. Amen.*

poison, it will not hurt them at all; they will place their hands on people who are ill, and they will get well.'

19After the Lord Jesus had spoken to them, he was taken up into heaven and he sat at the right hand of God. 20Then the disciples went out and preached everywhere, and the Lord worked with them and confirmed his word by the signs that accompanied it.

MARK'S THIRD GREAT QUESTION

We hope you've enjoyed reading Mark's account of the life of Jesus. Mark writes for a purpose. He wants to confront us with the questions: Who is Jesus? and: What did he achieve? He doesn't expect us just to read his book, enjoy it as an interesting piece of history, and then put it down and move on to something else. If it is true that Jesus lived... if Jesus really was God's Son... if Jesus really did rise again from the dead... then there is something we must do. Mark wants us to ask a third question: What must I do? How do we respond to this remarkable story?

It is possible, of course, that Jesus had an inflated sense of his own importance. People were certainly saying some amazing things about him. He was successful and popular.

> *Jesus and his disciples went on to the villages around Caesarea Philippi. On the way he asked them: "Who do people say I am?"*
> *They replied, "Some say John the Baptist; others say Elijah; and still others, one of the prophets."*
> *"But what about you?" he asked. "Who do you say I am?"*
> *Peter answered, "You are the Messiah."*

Mark 8:27-29 (see p.26)

The real Jesus

Hundreds of years previously, prophets had predicted that the "Messiah" would come to rescue those who put their trust in him. He would be born in Bethlehem, they said, come from a particular family, spend his life in Galilee, teach in parables and have God's power and authority.

For three years, Peter had seen Jesus perfectly fulfil these predictions. With a simple word or a touch, Jesus cured whole crowds of sick people, including the deaf, the blind and the disabled. Peter heard Jesus win arguments with the most brilliant minds of his age, silencing his critics and thrilling those who crowded round to hear his teaching.

Peter was there in the boat when Jesus commanded the storm to "be still", and it meekly obliged. On more than one occasion, Peter had seen Jesus take the hand of a corpse, and make the person live again.

But Peter knew there was more to Jesus than a miracle worker. He had never known anyone love like Jesus loved.

He saw Jesus' unique love for the outsiders, the downtrodden, the despised, the forgotten – those who no one else wanted to talk to, let alone love. Jesus treated women with a dignity unusual for his time and welcomed children with open arms.

Peter heard Jesus say: "Love your enemies and pray for those who persecute you". Later Jesus did just that – he prayed for his executioners: "Father, forgive them, for they do not know what they are doing".

Peter saw nothing strange about Jesus' repeated claims to be the one who forgives sins, the Lord of the Sabbath, the Son of the Blessed One… As far as he could see, these claims were justified – Jesus really was "the Messiah" – God in human form.

Nevertheless, there was something about Jesus that Peter and the other disciples had not yet understood…

The mission of Jesus

[Jesus] then began to teach them that the Son of Man must suffer many things and be rejected by the elders, the chief priests and the teachers of the law, and that he must be killed and after three days rise again. Mark 8:31 (see p.26)

Even those who make general statements about their own future often get it wrong. Margaret Thatcher, who became the British Prime Minister, once famously said: "I don't think that there will be a woman Prime Minister in my lifetime."

But Jesus could say exactly how he would die and who his killers would be, and predicted his return from death three days later.

More than that, Jesus knew that he "must" die. His death had a purpose which had been predicted hundreds of years before he was born. As Isaiah wrote, some 700 years previously:

He was pierced for our transgressions, he was crushed for our iniquities; the punishment that brought us peace was on him, and by his wounds we are healed. Isaiah 53:5

What does Isaiah mean by "our transgressions" and "our iniquities"?

The most important command

According to Jesus, the most important of God's commands is this: "Love the Lord your God with all your heart and with all your soul and with all your mind and with all your strength." God made us, he provides everything we need, and our response should be to love him – with everything we have.

But none of us have lived like that. Isaiah also wrote:

We all, like sheep, have gone astray, each of us has turned to our own way. Isaiah 53:6

We live as if we are the centre of the universe, not God. Jesus explains why we are like this:

"For it is from within, out of a person's heart, that evil thoughts come – sexual immorality, theft, murder, adultery, greed, malice, deceit, lewdness, envy, slander, arrogance and folly." Mark 7:21-23 (see page 22)

For whatever reason, we don't trust God to know what's best for us, so we choose to live life as if we're the boss. We ignore his rightful authority over our lives, and ignore his loving laws.

And the results of this rebellion are visible all around us. That's why relationships break down, the environment is polluted, communities are blighted by crime, war rages throughout the world, and terrorists destroy life as if it did not matter.

Because he is good, God will not let evil go unpunished, and treating God in the way we do is the most serious evil of all. It's what the Bible calls "sin".

Jesus is clear that sin results in death – eternal death, which he describes as "hell" (see Mark 9:42-48 on p.32). Jesus is very clear that people will be punished for all eternity if they die still rebelling against their Creator. The reason Jesus warns us about hell is because he loves us and does not want us to go there.

The perfect substitute

But amazingly, even though we have given up on God, God does not give up on us. Instead, he sent his Son to rescue us by dying for us. Jesus is not like a doctor who can tell us about the fatal disease we have but can do nothing to cure it. Jesus has the remedy for it – his death on the cross.

It was a death that had been predicted hundreds of years earlier, in remarkable detail: he would be… rejected by his own people; falsely accused but he would refuse to retaliate or speak up in his own defence; mocked and brutally beaten (although not one of his bones would be broken); executed with criminals, with spectators jeering at him and challenging God to rescue him. His killers would gamble for his clothes.

In all, twenty-nine such prophecies were fulfilled in the final twenty-four hours of Jesus' life. Jesus' death was not accidental. Neither was it pointless.

As he died, crying out: "My God, my God, why have you forsaken me?" Jesus was enduring the separation from God that each one of us deserves for our rebellion. He went through it so that we never have to, if only we will trust him.

That's why Jesus said that he "must" die.

Jesus died willingly so that we could be reconciled with our

Creator. He died as our substitute, in our place, taking the punishment we deserve.

> [Jesus said:] "For even the Son of Man did not come to be served, but to serve, and to give his life as a ransom for many." Mark 10:45 (see page 35)

Jesus' death was the ransom paid to set us free from sin and death.

The great escape

And when he rose from death three days later, just as he'd promised he would, Jesus proved that death had no power over him – or those who follow him.

The resurrection shows that Jesus is exactly who he claimed to be. It shows that his work of dying for our sins was an acceptable sacrifice to God. And those who follow Jesus have hope in the face of death because his resurrection opens up the gates of eternal life for anyone who will walk through them.

Eternal life is just as real and physical as life here now, but with one important difference – there will be no more sin.

And that means no more suffering, disease, fear, regrets, loneliness, unfulfilled dreams or death. Jesus promises those who follow him that they will "have life, and have it to the full". This is why Jesus came.

But what about that third question? What must I do? Jesus himself tells us how we must respond...

The cost of following Jesus

> [Jesus said:] "Whoever wants to be my disciple must deny themselves and take up their cross and follow me. For whoever wants to save their life will lose it, but whoever loses their life for me and for the gospel will save it. What good is it for someone to gain the whole world, yet forfeit their soul?" Mark 8:34-36 (see p.29)

If we choose to follow Jesus, we have everything to gain: "Whoever loses their life for me and for the gospel will save it". God's Spirit will come to live in us, we'll be forgiven, we'll enjoy a deep sense of peace, joy, purpose and freedom, and we'll know for certain that we have eternal life.

Restored to the relationship with God that we were created for, we can finally begin to live as we were meant to live.

But, if we choose to follow Christ, we also have much to lose: "Whoever wants to be my disciple must deny themselves and take up their cross and follow me".

Following Jesus means "denying self": turning away from selfish instincts; living for God – and for others – rather than ourselves; supporting Jesus' priorities for ourselves and the world, and rejecting what Jesus is against.

Following Jesus also means "taking up our cross": it means being prepared to suffer and face opposition for his sake.

Living like that may cost us dearly in terms of our friends, family, popularity, wealth and work. But, as Jesus reminds us, what is the point of having all those things if they cost us the most valuable thing we have? "What good is it for someone to gain the whole world," says Jesus, "yet forfeit their soul?"

If you suffer for following Christ, you still have the most precious thing in the world: the joy of knowing God, the peace of his forgiveness, the company of God's worldwide family, and the certainty of eternal life.

Your response

People respond to Jesus in many different ways. Some choose to ignore him, some deliberately reject him, and others try to put off the decision until later.

But Jesus – this man of unmatched power, authority, integrity and love – reminds us that there are consequences to the choices we make: "Whoever wants to save their life will lose it, but whoever loses their life for me and for the gospel will save it". Jesus calls us to follow him. Don't close your mind and heart to what he is saying.

Think about the **identity** of Jesus. Who do you think he is?
Think about the **mission** of Jesus. What did he come to do?
Think about the **call** of Jesus. What does he want you to do?

When you have thought about these things for a moment, read the next section for some suggestions on how you can make your own personal response to the Gospel of Mark.

HOW DO I RESPOND TO JESUS?

- **Find out more.** You may still have many questions, so why not join a *Christianity Explored* course near you, where you can discover more about Jesus and the Christian message in an informal and relaxed way? Visit www.christianityexplored. org and click on "The CE Course" to find out more information or to be put in touch with someone running a course in your area. You won't be asked to read aloud, pray or sing. You can ask any question you like – or you can just sit and listen.

- **Read a book.** You could try another Gospel such as Luke or John and start to think more deeply about the questions that Mark poses: Who is Jesus? Why did he come? What does it mean to follow him? For some great answers to common questions and other helpful resources, visit www. christianityexplored.org

- **Visit a church** where the Bible is taught and clearly explained. There, you will meet other people who are asking and trying to answer the same questions you are. You will be helped by the teaching, and be encouraged and supported by the other members. A good place to start would be to ask the person who gave you this Gospel for some advice.

- **Talk to God – pray.** Talk to him about what you have discovered as you have read the Gospel of Mark and thought about Jesus' life, teaching and death. Thank God for Jesus and what he means to you. You can speak freely to God in your own words, because God looks into our hearts and understands our real longings – even if our words are hesitant and uncertain. You may still have many questions, but talk to God about them, and ask for his help to grow in your understanding. Tell him that you are sorry that you have not loved him with all your heart, soul, mind and strength. Tell him that you want to serve King Jesus in the same way he has served us. Ask him to help you change.

Map of places in
MARK'S GOSPEL

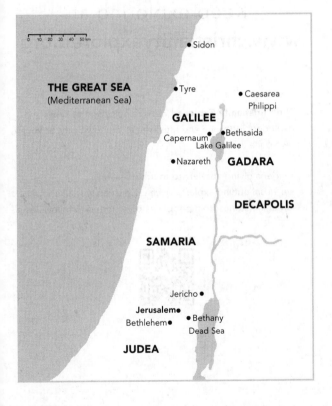

0 10 20 30 40 50 km

THE GREAT SEA
(Mediterranean Sea)

● Sidon

● Tyre

● Caesarea
Philippi

GALILEE

Capernaum ● ● Bethsaida
Lake Galilee

● Nazareth   **GADARA**

DECAPOLIS

SAMARIA

Jericho ●

Jerusalem ●
Bethlehem ● ● Bethany
Dead Sea

JUDEA

Keep exploring at
www.christianityexplored.org

The **Christianity Explored** website helps you to keep exploring Jesus' life and message in your own way, at your own pace. It features:

• videos giving answers to tough questions.
• a visual outline explaining what Christianity is all about.
• real-life stories from people who've started to follow Jesus.